chicano blood transfusion

chicano blood transfusion

EDWARD VIDAURRE

FLOWERSONG BOOKS

DONNA, TX

ISBN 10: 0692411461
ISBN 13: 978-0692411469

FlowerSong Books
4717 N FM 493
Donna, TX 78537
www.flowersongbooks.com

First printed edition: March 2016

Contents

"There is no one Chicano language just as there is no one Chicano experience."

—Gloria E. Anzaldúa

"Raise your words, not voice. It is rain that grows flowers, not thunder."

—Rumi

In Memory of
Eloy A. Romero

y

Francisco X. Alarcón

Dedicated to
Liliana Ramírez

Luisa Isabella Vidaurre

The Poets Responding to SB1070

Odilia, Sharon, Iris, y Sonia

Daniel García Ordaz and family

A special thank you to
Mario Godínez for this amazing cover art

Gemini Ink for all that you do

My friends in the RGV of South Texas

100 Thousand Poets for Change

Acknowledgements

Agradacimiento profundo to the editors of the following publications for publishing poems in this collection:

La Bloga
University of Arizona Press
Lamar University Press
VAO Publishing
Bordersenses
Interstice-South Texas College
Brooklyn & Boyle
Harbinger Asylum
El Zarape Press
The Monitor
Left Hand Of The Father
La Noria Literary Journal
Poets Responding to SB1070
riverSedge: A Journal of Art and Literature, UTRGV
Voices de la Luna: A Quarterly Poetry & Arts Magazine
McAllen Arts Council
Valley Morning Star
Lazy Fascist

PART ONE

25 to Life

My poetry is serving a life sentence
For crimes against
Love
Imagery
Structure
Meaning
Y translation

It was judged by 12
And will be carried out by six
Six poets
One with her head buried in an oven
Searching for a burnt-out stanza
Another with beer in hand
Spitting out profanities to
A headless horse at a racetrack
And four others because society
Les indicó que paren

My poetry
Sleeps on a cold bed
Made of steel
Next to a leaky sink
Que gotea las 24 horas

It's written behind
Chipped bars that need
A paint touch-up
That keep it down
That don't forgive
Y nunca abren

It was caught breaking
Making holes in a wall
That if made
Would have inspired
It to be poems
Of freedom
Poems for its people
Poems of justice
Poems
chingones

It waits patiently
For its lethal
Ink-jection now

One day
And when that day comes
My poetry will be free
My poetry will be legal
Mi poesía cantará

Until then
It serves a life sentence
¡Por ser
Chicano!

Los Desaparecidos

Perseus with the head of Medusa (Mujer Zeta decapitada por el Cartel del Golfo)
Oil on linen 7ft tall by 5 1/2 feet wide. 2014 by Rigoberto A. Gonzalez

Everyone has the gift of invisibility,
even the border wall goes unnoticed in June after a
month that drains us of life. The scent of knives
on a hot summer is the only constant
amongst the news of frontera tragedies and a poetry
reading in a stick-to-your-skin humid bar in a small South Texas town.

We all have the gift of going missing,
like the breath of a collapsing lung,
like a whisper from behind, a shooting star.
Or do we just hide reading a newspaper upside-down
when the new Sheriff arrives?

Puede ser que también los periódicos se convierten
en lanchas que se lanzan en un rio olvidado, en aguas
color a sangre de tantos que casi por las yemas de los dedos
tocaban tierra estadounidense.

The missing,
they recite "Howl" across the Rio Grande
but not the Ginsberg lament for his brethren
but the howls of suffering souls crammed in stash houses
across our children's playgrounds, those left
for dead in sweltering sardine packed vessels—
those left alive to remember hell is real.

Los desaparecidos
quieren ser encontrados
aún decapitados y sin lenguas.
Siguen gritando porque el silencio es fuerte en sufrimiento.

We will keep them alive and find them!
Through art, poetry, music, stories that scare the night,
and lullabies that make our children sleep tight.

Cuando los cantos se vuelven agua
el olor de cuchillos en el aire
bailan con la buganvilla trepadora
descendiéndose seis pies bajo la tierra sin nombre——
sólo una alabanza que fluye entre la tierra agrietada.

*cuando los cantos se vuelven agua: Martín Espada——gracias por la inspiración

4 | edward vidaurre

Stray bullet #1

Slow dancing

                       a gunshot

  is heard

                        Eyes meet

     in Autumn

Borde Bermellón

veiled threat
on which fights jump off
into city streets,
mass transit, supermercado chants,
y tendederos

despacito,
sending lips into seclusion
making soft sounds
extinct

lips,
ode to dandelion
seeds exploding in air,
ode to frowns
haciendo muecas,
ode to songs
lip-synced,
ode to gritos
across colonias,
ode to last breaths

words get stuck behind
teeth, like teclas on
máquinas de escribir

labios que cuentan
historias, cantan canciones,
besan dolores, that make
love by just pushing
words into existence.

Lágrimas (hojas)

a mi arbolito se le caen las lágrimas
(hojas)

a mi arbolito nadie se le acerca
(verano)

a mi arbolito nadie le habla
(solitario)

a mi arbolito se le caen las lágrimas
(otoño)

mi arbolito tiene música
(cenzontle)

a mi arbolito le llegó visita
(gato)

a mi arbolito se le fue la música
(brisa tosca)

mi arbolito sigue su llanto
(hojas)

Siguanaba

Soñé tus manos,
Siguanaba
sentí tu besos,
Siguanaba,

de lejos te vi pasar,
macihuatli,
a mis narices llegó tu aliento,
macihuatli,

escuché que me hablabas,
Siguanaba,
sobre el río frío te vi desnuda,
Siguanaba,

era una noche sin luna,
era una noche sin cara,

Macihuatli.

On Growing Old without Grace

you sometimes swallow
watermelon seeds and drink
milk straight from the bottle

afraid of pepper sticking
to your liver and eat flour

tortillas. Take up pipe
smoking and try recollecting
stories from years back, yet

can't find the TUMS. Shine shoes,
keep the same ritual for drinking
coffee—extra sugar and lots of cream.

you spend more time combing
less hair and less time bathing.
you think doctors are wrong, umpires
make bad calls, food is bland, politicians

don't care and swear you
had more money in the bank

not even the shaking of your hands
can convince you that the end is near

you can still strap on your boots
and make a half-Windsor

Stray bullet #2

Silence turned to

                                   rust,

One   sound,
loose chain on bike

                              —smoke from

9mm.
A crying

               ambulance nears.

Hermano

Leaves on the retama
have been gone for a while now
as has my brother, who left behind

his pants on the mesquite
branches just under
la baya de muérdago y anacua.

Where did you go, hermano?

Was it you who ate from
the prickly pear? Was it your blood
I saw on the concrete slab
near the cattle crossing beyond
the chaparral? Did you

drink from the sultry air
when you got thirsty
and the hunger pangs set in?

I'll be back soon, leave me
your water bottles, even if
empty.

** Flash Nature Writing Workshop for Poets, Writers, Artists, Sketcheristas and
Photographers: January 19, 2014*

Un Camino

—after Langston Hughes' poem "One-Way Ticket"

Abrazo mi vida
y me la llevo conmigo
y la dejo en
Honduras, El Salvador,
En Guatemala y
Cualquier lugar que es
Norte o Oeste—

Abrazo mi vida
y me la llevo en La Bestia
desde Chiapas
entre cemento y maíz,
trigo y el diésel
Cualquier lugar que es
Norte o Este—
Pero no pal' Sur

¡Estoy harto!
Con las muertes,
Gente cruel
con miedo,
que matan y corren,
me tienen miedo
Y yo también a ellos.

Abrazo mi vida
Y me la llevo
Un boleto de un camino—
Me voy pal' Oeste,
Me voy pal' Norte,
Me voy.

Closer

para mi madre

closer,
to your bosom
para cuando me de sed
allí en el pezón me emborracho
—al cerrar los ojos

closer,
my little voice has a secret

closer,
to your arthritic huesos
para cuando me falte valor
alli entre carne y huella gritare
—victorioso

closer
cramp-your-style closeness

closer,
to smell your hair
para cuando las flores mueran en el invierno
allí entre vello y cráneo pensare
—brillante

closer,
muggy, bien cerquita

closer,
to hear your breathing
para cuando el dolor de quebrantados de corazón me trage
allí con tu suspiro
—me vuelvo a restablecer

closer,
—overwhelming

así es, madrecita
empalagoso como
too much of anything

—bendito a tu alcance

Trapped Between Mahogany, La Joya, TX

2,000 miles
trapped between mahogany.
Truths, lies, and wonder
jump in and out
of streams. Headless
bodies crawling into
bushes, fires, and frigid
unwelcoming rivers and oceans.

2,000 miles
alone, Ignored, banned, deported,
detained and spotted. Observed behind
iron gates and fences. Shackled in stash houses,
sinking in ships and sprayed by low flying
pesticide spitting drones

2,000 miles
sold, rented & borrowed
never to return
never to be found
only to be replaced
burned, buried and forgotten.

2,000 miles
a phone number, a belt,
black leather boots, and a white rosary
with bloody beads

confirms: Elvis has left the border

Pueblo del Sol, Boyle Heights

Impoverished heaven
with stories of fallen chol@s
with worn out cartilage

On summer nights
we forgot we were poor
as the Krylon fumes melted our senses
in brown paper bags

We played down the line
jumped on rooftops
—swam across concrete jungles

Your voice silenced
by cries
at a distance
in the bushes of clay hills

you let me live through
crooked alleys
and fall in love
with girls with slanted smiles
y fertile wombs
bodies embraced behind
torn curtain silhouettes

Isolated from the City of Angels
gangs ruled the concrete landscape

Stray bullet #3

Corridos play,
en la cocina
Mamá stirs el caldo

en la sala
la más chiquita falls into
her tea set: she serves

blood to her dolls.

Los Tres Sans

Luis Alfonso (Santa Ana, El Salvador)

Ayer vi policias
federales
with their faces half
covered in black mesh
with only their souls in view

today *abuelito*
me acuerdo como
te tapabas la boca para
tocer y las lágrimas que
formaban en tus ojos
del dolor
y tú, sonriendo con toda tu
fuerza como decir
'no te preocupes, estoy bien'

I remember

Roberto Vargas (Los Angeles y San Francisco, Califas)

amigo de infancia
I still rememeber you
riding up in your motorcycle
with the needle on *'Échale'*
tu casco
lleno de insectos
después de la manejada
desde San Pancho

abrazándote and drinking
cold beers
while we laughed and joked in the
concrete jungle of our youth

Ray Ramirez Jr. (San Benito, Texas)

Aquí estoy
en tu pueblo
de San Bene
cruising the hoods
and waving at unknown
peeps down Freddy Fender Lane
breathing the air that once
owned your grin and pleasured
itself from your mesquite smoke
that billowed out of the pits on Batts

Aquí estoy
in this small community
of poets, politicians, musicians
and a hangover from your passing

Tu nieta te conoció,
te conoce, y nunca te olvidara
como las tantas personas
de tu pueblito
near the *Resaca*
of wasted days
and wasted nights.

Lorca in the Barrio

(ode to "Lorca's Fable" and "Round of the Three Friends")

Travieso,
Chepe,
Lalo

the three of them frozen:
Travieso by the world of bullets;
Chepe by the world of syringes and acid trips;
Lalo by the marching of monks through his barrio.

Travieso,
Chepe,
Lalo

the three of them burned:
Travieso by the world of pigeon shit and chalk outlines;
Chepe by the world of drive by shootings and rucas with feathered hair;
Lalo by the world of banned literature and dead lecturers.

Travieso,

Chepe,
Lalo,
the three of them buried:
Travieso in Lupitas tattoo;
Chepe in the carga going through his bloodstream:
Lalo in the roosters crow, the dog's howl, and the glossy eyes
of his tecato father.

Lalo,

Chepe,

Travieso,

the three in my hands were

three Zoot Suit scholars,

three crooked cops,

three birds of different races and a Autumn spirits

that flew around landing in blood stained sidewalks being outlined by

death.

Uno

y uno

y uno,

los tres enterrados,

con la ternura del Invierno,

con la tinta negra de palabras escritas antes del suicido de la Primavera,

con las lágrimas de Sofía que espera ser realidad en el útero del Verano,

por la miel que llora la Luna hace el triste

    mar en Otoño.

Three

y dos

y uno,

I saw them run, hide and die

on the streets of Los Angeles

into a dark alley,

into the night of anxiety filled smog,

into the voiceless screams and anguish of their mother's

    open mouths.

into my sadness of domestic abuse and alcoholism,
into the bar with the velvet curtain,
into my own death unannounced last year.

I killed the last of the Chicano writers
and a few people in Arizona held their champagne flutes in the air.
While Menchita tucked in their little wonderful children to the tune of
La llorona, breathing over them.
Travieso,
Chepe,
Lalo.

Chicanas are hard,
but sometimes if you lay your head,
between their soft breasts you can hear the cries of a new generation
of raza with the knowledge and power to make a man shit in fear,
y eso me conforma

Cuando ya no pude ver las luces de la ambulancia
pasando la loma sobre la calle Cesar Chávez
entendí que me asesinaron también a mi.
Esa noche en el barrio destaparon todas las sábanas blancas
buscándome entre las caras fallecidas, en las iglesias, los panteones,
callejones, y las aguas del rio frio.
Still they couldn't find me.
¿No pudieron?
No they couldn't.

Sin balas en mi cuete,
pero con un libro y lápiz en mi mano,
empecé a escribir poemas...

Valley Girl

She's a WiFi hotspot,
a real page-turner,
lips with erotic stories,
a beauty on the outer edges
of my retina, soft
—a diva

She's happily-ever-after
Fantasies carved out of mesquite
With sunflower hair,
Chasing dreams on the back
Of a javalina
—near resacas

She's pucker-lipped,
Red-dawn toughness,
Boot-strapped,
Scuffmark tattoos on her
Breasts that heave
—with the sound of accordions

She's downtown,
Corner street,
Red-light special
A fishnet stocking mess
—tumblin' out of Lopez bar
With lipstick smeared
By who knows who

She's chilaquilles
After midnight
Triangle cut
—corn tortillas
hot and melted
Over the top

She's country
Jeans, beer, gum chewing
Mollejas dorada,
Chamoyada y raspas
White Wing shooter
—a Valley girl

Stash House in My Heart

Cramming regrets y
traición into the wounded

part de mi corazón
—wounded, but beating

you don't see beyond
your own pain, heartbreaker

asking for a ransom
but you already took all

I had, y más. Todo
Everything.

quit dreaming, the grass
is blue on the other side

you abandoned us
love don't live here anymore

Wall 2

Bella asked me to draw her a wall.
A wall? I drew a square. She said it didn't look like a wall. I thought
about it. It seemed so simple. I never thought a wall could be so
complicated. So I thought of things that associate with a wall. The things
that hang from it, what's on the other side of it, etc.
A wall.
Does it own a color?
Does it divide nations?
Does it have ridges to hold while being climbed?
Does it have a name?
Does it have a purpose?
Does it heal?
Does it have a theme song?
If I get to the top, will I want to come back down?
Will I be forced down? Or will I be stopped short of reaching the top?
A wall.
It's complicated. It's oppressing. If I knock it down, will freedom ring?

The Power of Positive Thinking

"look at the bright side of things"
you'll die, eventually. But not alone
—you'll take with you the winter solstice
and song from the crickets when they breathe.

"How do I know this?"
simple, In September when my father
died he took with him the smell of alguashte
and the taste of semita

Things are never the same. They just
change. So because you love the first day of winter
and the breathing of crickets, they too will go on living.
Just not here.

Just don't love me much,
or the sound of pages turning,
the scent of ink or the sound of
dueling violins.

No one has the right to those.

Poetry Has Left Me

"Little escorts"
that's all it says on my notepad.
Was it the beginning of a poem?
A joke? A new reality show?

I woke up at 5:06am
in Falfurrias, shared some
birthday cake with some trucker
friends of friends
beneath me, the earth gasped

"House lizard"
another random writing
on my notepad

Randy Travis got me
through a small town seven
miles short of Refugio

Woke up to Bread
to my right,
a horse
alone, welcoming a new day
then I drift off again

I remember my sisters taking turns
brushing their long hair
in front of the tele watching
a novela

Gloria Trevi was Almita's
Madonna
and I wore khakis, Ben Davis
shirts and still didn't
know how to properly
inhale smoke from a cigarette,

Fresh fruit for sale,
a dead dog, and a river
with a name I couldn't make out
is what I saw last
before waking up on Decatur.

Stray bullet #4

Evergreen,
Dry earth and silence,
At a distance, a sob
Six feet under

—bones shift

Bus 31

Las puertas no se abren
Levanto mi mano
Enseñándole mi boleto
Al conductor

Adentro
Veinte pasajeros, todos
Con llanto en los ojos
Sin boca, sin destino

Entre ellos
Un niño
Con camisa blanca
Sin ojos, canicas en las manos
Gritando que lo dejen
Bajar.

Ode to the Paletero Who Robbed Me

pushing ice like weight
el paletero
at a distance
empujando la hielera con llantas
sus pies ladeados
zapatos chuecos
cachucha de los Doyers
camisa manga larga
prieto, ojos color café
la campanita
ring' ring' ring'
de coco, de sandía
strawberry-flavored too
metí la mano
sacó el filero
Swatch watch
coolin' on his wrist
as I ran away with a watch tan line
towards the first-street bridge

Stray bullet #5

She swings the rebozo
Over her head, dressed in black
primer luto del otoño
she hides behind the color black

Down the Line

Swinging at bruised leather baseballs and trying to keep it between second and third base. Barrio rules. We were latch-key kids living near four miles south of Dodger Stadium, or, as the older *veteranos* in the neighborhood called it, Chavez Ravine. They claim the *gobierno* came down on the landowners who were Mexican-American and took their *pedazo* of the American Dream. Why? I don't know, but it never stopped them from wearing blue-and-white *"doyer"* caps and being proud when *"Fernandomania"* took the baseball world by storm.

You already knew who would win, who would hope to win, and who would struggle. *Chepito* would struggle most. He bent and hunched over the plate and always swung late, making sure the ball would go foul or down the line in the wrong direction. These were the rules plain and simple. For *Chepito* the game was hard and complicated. Then there was Juan, square-jawed, muscular: *"el mero mero honronero."* His brothers were all athletes—even his beautiful sister, Maria could outrun us. We would all pause and wait to see how far he could hit the ball. All the *chavalitos* would run past the center-fielder—back, back, back where it would be gone.

The bully gang-bangers rode around in "borrowed" bicycles with cigarettes hanging from their lips as the stillness of summer allowed for an inch of ash to hang from their pubescent hairline moustaches. The girls sat at a distance while the boys glanced over, trying to hit the ball into the gap at left-center, showing off, yelling loudly with their off-key mini machismo selves. I sat watching the *homies* making memories in my mind, sipping on a cream soda until it was my turn to bat. We played hard and tattooed sweat marks on our t-shirts, making spider web designs across our backs. Some of us had plastic gloves with half our hands sticking out and some had the leather mitts that were passed down from their older siblings with spit stains, and—if they were lucky—a Steve Garvey autograph.

If you hit the ball between right-center it would carry towards the cafeteria of the school grounds where we played after the last employee left for the day. Not too far from where I tasted my first kiss from Chicana lips, moist and strange—her tongue confused me into manhood, making me *firme* after rounding second with the prettiest girl I knew.

Down the line, down the streets, *curvas* thrown at us—life always trying to count us out. We played until the first call from our mothers rang through the barrio, until the sun abandoned us, until the gunshots sounded, or until Vin Scully's voice was tuned down on the television to listen to the radio broadcast of Jaime Jarrin's voice translating the game known to us as *beisbol.*

I Was Born by the River

In a dying county hospital
with perfect corners
wailing mothers, blue-lung
nurses and burger-eating dieticians.

I was born by the river

where my first kiss came from
a curious girl, with a curious smile,
a curious soul and a curious life
on a curious sofa

I was born five years after a dream

The Netherlands got color
and a temporary hold was put
on a drum major for peace
for righteousness
while a crook entered
the presidential race

I was born by the river

where inner tubes floated
on by, under the bridge
adjacent to the concrete *selvas*
where east meets west
where cheese is free

and we celebrated a champion
by taking the day off from school
to sleep in a bit longer and dream

But I know a change gon' come

Beat-Rotica

Your hair is soft
soft and splendid
sometimes i wish there was no God
to know all my thoughts
to know of my thoughts   the things i would do to you
the nerve of me   selfish
self-taught in the ways of sinful pleasures
i want to learn them with you
i want to forget about the moon with you
the moon frowns and the stars die

it was the brick and post   it was walking fast past the voodoo shops
it was the chicory   it was the jazz
it was fifty two degrees   it was definitely the jazz

it had to be the jazz   it was the voodoo we found in the alley
underneath the emergency staircase
it was the lipstick smeared on my chest
the things i would do to you

splendid like the face of death
right before the orgasm of our shadows
like the orgasm of hollywood and vine   the nerve of me
again the moon shines   and again it dies   again we forget

it was the palm trees swaying
it was the open mouth of the coming sea
it was the sun
it was poetry
it was smoggy and overcast
it was definitely the poetry
it had to be the words

it was the kiss from your lips
the hard-on you left behind   on them boys
their imagination of your lips   on what you left behind

again the moon rises   and dies   and is forgotten
the stars die   it was this poem
erotic and selfish   turning heads   giving blowjobs in the rain
it was your lips   falling from the sky
gasping to die before the land
slowly praying before it lands
on the pages
of time

we sit across from each other
with the grains in our mouths
of coffee from the french press
waiting for the first word
to come out of our filthy mouths

a song of sadness a song of sexual intercourse   of course
a song of sex   a song that will die
along with the moon and the stars

Stray bullet #6

We	danced
there was a	blast
the music	stopped
there was a	screeching sound
her hazel eyes	saw the light

To Live and Die in L.A.

"I want to be known for my love of feeding ants, and cats and my poetry"
—Rose Sanchez, a homegirl from Guadalupe, AZ

I want to be known for trying   I want to be known for believing
for what it's worth
Let's all get on the bus   make memories   ride it to downtown
get off where the crime is high   the smell of homelessness   is thick
where the earth breaks heels   dreams get shattered   hope is face-
down on a puddle   inches from the gutter   drain solstice   dream-
catchers hang from the cutlass supreme   pristine   low- ridin'
Broadway   then comes the night   silent   guns cocked
oldies play   guitar riffs and cigarette smoke   both drive
upward   squeeze the soul   with serrano chiles   lick lips until red
-chapped   lose another friend to gang violence   graffiti name on
wall   feel blue   feel lucky   drink beer   pour it out on the
crying asphalt   slower than usual   usual routine   evergreen
reminisce   let's get off the bus   next stop   death and the bus ride
home   run through clothes hangers inhaling the honesty   run home
chiles rellenos roasting on gas stove   wash hands   run back down
I stand alone   me, a dove
and a crow   a bullet piercing through my gut   slippin' into my
brown soul   chalk outlines   Aliso Village 1991

42 | edward vidaurre

PART TWO

Something inside rages with music.
Como quetzal, aguantas la humedad de
las tierras altas. Something inside
calms the sea. Como león, te desapareces.

Something inside is holding back the wind.
Como corazón del cielo, nacido entre aguas
turbulentas. Something looks out. Everything

sneaks in, like the moon through the windowpane

Lips of a Chola

I sat in the back seat
cruisin' down Saviers Rd.
1991, Oxnard, CA

She had dark brown eyes
that would frighten
anyone else but
me that night

Her Monte Carlo
dipped and swerved
I just sat back and smiled

I kept my gaze on the rear view
mirror, as images of her
dark eyeshadow and lips traded places

the bass from the music
along with the yesca
in my system made
her lips that much more gorgeous
the lips of a chola are amazing

they glistened
they promised
they told stories

I felt the distance
between us unreachable

the lips of a chola are amazing

I wanted hers
but her friend was on my lap

her lips,
not so soft

Calaveras

I.

you died entirely
without me, taking with you
the colors of your small town, its music
and dusty roads. Your hand swept the streets
from the tracks where you walked—and the sounds
of the deep shadowy night. I've grieved in front of
a mirror that doesn't reflect, that only bounces off the echo
of my grieving heart. You picked your destiny, I
picked to wait for a sign from the prideful sun.
I stare, destroyed
—alone wearing your lips.

2.

I sin best during days of obligation. I pray for the neighbors' mesquite
tree to come crashing down on the lawn mower that roars on hangover
Sunday. My favorite coffee mug has become the pool for the paint
brushes my daughter uses to draw sad faces on recycled robots. Life, a
sigh. I mourn the death of an unknown man, handsome with fists the
size of watermelons and lips of bronze. My favorite t-shirt has become a
dust rag. The vacuum has a bad cough and will not come out this
weekend. Stop faking a smile, your lips will stay that way.

3.

Touch the hands of the dead. I promise, you will never be afraid of their
ghost if you do. I did, and the ghost followed me through blow-job alley
and broken syringe boulevard. It lifted my eyelids in the middle of the
night to show me its wounds. It covered my 300 pound body in a bat
skin pall. It sang me songs that if spoken became poems read in
cemeteries where black crows go to die singing "my home's in hell."

4.

The month I met you,
there was an earthquake and tsunami in Vanuatu.

The month I moved in with you,
a scallop dredger sunk due to heavy storms.

The month I married you,
a fab four died - cancer

The month our child was born,
there was a festival on the Isle of Man,

The month we separated,
children played around carved pumpkins.

The month I fell in love with you,
an acoustic-guitar-driven ballad which tells
of the end of a romance topped the charts.

5.

one day,
there will be no me,
no shadow of me,
no breath in me,
no snoring giant at your side,
just an impression that lingers
like the moment after an earthquake,
—bewilderment
yeah that's it!
a fuckin' daze!

chicano blood transfusion

I got shot in the gut
and now I need
a Chicano blood transfusion.

Make sure the vials come from the underground.

Quick!

alurista is coming down the corridor and wants my hat for his collection

What for the rush and bloody pain
What for the blooming and the rain

Close the door! Put a sheet over my body and tag my toe.
My brown skin is hindered by the loss of blood.

Help! Minute Men are looking for me,
la migra is banging on my door!
La chota has me surrounded
In hand, pistolas with hairline triggers,

I can hear them approaching with
their steel- toed boots crushing
the concrete up the piss stained staircase.
breaking out the chalk, ready to outline me
for being a Voice

Where's the sangre?
I'm losing consciousness
strap Juan Felipe Herrera down
—take it from him

cause' I can only come up with 180 reasons why a Guanaco can't cross
the border.

Look for the descendants of
"Corky" Gonzales

who also is the blood,
the image of myself.

Ask a Chicana in the midst
with beautiful brown eyes,
to hold my hand during the
mezcla of Pupil y Maya

I can't write anymore, my pen is missing
along with my grandma's recipe for champurrado y chiles rellenos.

I need those to help me break
through the concrete wall mierda stretching from Califas to Tejas.

I worry about my citizenship/permiso para jalar/needing a haircut on
        Sundays
I worry about people that drive small cars/con placas vencidas/con
        placas behind them

STOP!

Alright I think it's done
I feel the same

Chingón!
Guanaco!
Chicano!

Angeleno!
Tejano!

With the blood of
Mi gente del barrio

Guión

do you know the in-between?

I do

I plank on hyphens

there I understand the reason for lighting candles

there I read banned music notes

there lorca explains duende to me

there oldies teach me the meaning behind quinceañera dance

choreography

there I can see mi gente running and jumping over la pobreza into el

racismo

there our children are detained

there clouds come down and carry off my denials

there I search for the chemical reaction that makes love work

there is where Neruda dropped his pen after asking for silence

there the CIA jumped off

there lie the odes yet written

there goes an ode for the unwritten

there revolutions rise

there a poem lies face down

there

between the hyphen

there

right there

Tejidos

She's back again. Always in the early
evenings. Shrouded in white, she kneads
the hollow under my ribcage. A soft moan
escapes me. a hot breath whispers. The
void open its mouth. It swallows invitingly.
I stand on its ledge looking down.
Should I or shouldn't I?

"The Visitor"
—Gloria Anzaldúa

From the womb of a Salvadoreña
I was born trucha!

I'm a shoeless
child running around the neighborhood
watching pigeons and
drinking water
from a moldy hose
watching my neighbor's sister
hang dry her bra

I'm a huerco 27 years
separated from Tejas
with its Valley of Trechas
y catan-filled resaca shores

I'm a tagger
defacing bus windows
—a 4-year-old eating boogers
and a 17-year-old
tasting Chicana lips in the dark

Julio Cesar, Lalo G.,
Corky and the Young Lords——
those are the Chicanos.

I am not

I am a poet
Who stays trucha

Stray bullet #7

Butterfly suicides

in October—
a breeze gives them an extra push

into the SUV

Last Day on the Calendar

I will name her Mayahuel
Because it flows
Off my tongue,
Like honey.

I will name her Cenzontle
Because it flies
From my hands,
Like failure.

I will name him Maxtla
Because I lost
Everything I worked hard for,
Like language

I will name him Tlaloc
Because I'm famished
and we stopped picking crops
To enjoy the petrichor

Together with them
We will settle in Huehue Tlapallan
Feeding each other and them
Fire from the sun...and wait for
Death by suffocation.

A Girl from Michoacán

Let our voices be heard,
The golden hymns of our soul

I.

Her small town vanished
Bending the corner, leaving a dusty trail
Teocaltiche, en Los Altos de Jalisco

II.

Calor en Aguascalientes
¡Ardiente!
She hung on
bus overturned
Fifty four bodies bashed against one another
Nuestra hermana and twelve survived

III.

Her Mother, brown
Her Sun, brown
Her Womb, brown
Zacatecas, was brown

IV.

Forty three men
Six women
Will never think again
Will never dream again
Will never speak again
Will never see the brown Sun
Ever again

*decapitated bodies found

V.

She was close,
Her knees bleeding,
head bent forward,
869 km después
5 more to go
She closed her eyes and remembered
Her small town
A chapulín crosses her path
As she becomes one
With the sun

¡Justicia!

I wanted to write a love poem,
but the cries of slaughtered rabbits
made me write of border violence.

I wanted to write a poem about a serene river,
but the dark waters reflected the faces
of newly orphaned children trapped in a stash house
begging to die amongst the monarch butterflies.

I almost wrote a poem about hate,
instead I picked up a knife and
tore through every tree
in Texas, leaving nothing but
a sap and blood trail.

I wanted to write a poem to a child,
but twenty voices cried out, "That's not fair!"
Instead, I watched my daughter eat
ice cream as I spoke to her
in a whisper about angels.

I wanted to write a poem about growing up,
but my mother's tears dripping into the caldo de res,
the soft humming of the refrigerator and the blank pages
on the coffee table stunted all growth.

I wrote a poem about survival—
¡JUSTICIA!
is her name

Breaking the Wall

You can see my ghetto through the gaps in my mouth, teeth separated to let the light in. You can hear the pleading and angry fist pumping minority chants of freedom ringing. You can lick my skin and taste the red clay of yesterday and finger my scars of lashes for not wanting blue eyed mensitas, it's the pain inflicted because we preferred our own, moren@s con pelitos en los brazos. Who said brown wasn't beautiful? Who said long black straight hair and chicana lips were not delicious? Who said our dialect was lacking phonetic acceptance? We killed the whale first, and stepped on the queen ant. We build until we can't recognize our hands so that our future generation will never forget their past. We discovered love and you generated disease. You drew out a border wall, and we're gonna knock that bitch down.

Luna Roja

peaches were being served on the moon last night
it was chilly there, with a light snow falling
even still, you walked on her soft skin, bare-breasted
running towards mountains where she is about to give
birth to new stars, where darkness is buried,
where trees have baby leaves that speak in crisp whispers:
that teach you poetry
that make your eyes appreciate art
that tell you of its history
that tell you of two hundred ways to use your lips
tomorrow, peaches will be served again
it will be the first day of spring, you will sing
naked, running towards fresh spring water,
i will be there on my knees waiting,
ready to instruct your thighs to descend
along with the blue moon

Cover Them

Cover them in whispers
Cover them in caliche
Cover them, and sprinkle nopales
Over their grave
To our sisters,
You whisper white lies
You grab their nalgas
You promise pendejadas
Take your boots, they were
Made for walking
But you use them to step on our
Accents and broken backs
Kick our wages under the flag
My mother once told me
"A los gringos les vale madre"
But I fell in love with blue eyes once
With power and privilege
Cover them in whispers
Of sorries
Because one day they will
Catch me, scatter me across
Stolen land, in the grave
I'll cry out until my bones shatter
Until the world ends in fire
Cover them in whispers
Cover them and walk away
Wearing their boots.

cover them in whispers of sorries, line from "Suicide Note" by Janice Mirikitani

La Chota

after Pat Mora's "La Migra"

I.

Let's play La Chota
I'll be the policeman
You be the black kid.
I get the baton and stun gun.
You just walk away with your back to me,
I have a gun, though
I'll shoot for no reason: the badge protects ME. But first I'll beat you
And maybe cut off your breathing with a choke hold. But first I'll count
to ten and let you run.

II.

Let's play La Chota
I'll be your child
Wearing a hoodie
With my back to you
I'll have headphones on
I won't hear you say "freeze"

Summer Fruit

I was going 75 mph on a two-way street north of Edinburg. "Right there!" she said. It was a white pick-up truck filled with watermelons. There is always one watermelon cut in half with a knife stuck in it, the sampler. We drove a bit further, a long stretch of dry earth with sunflower petal remains that covered the eyes of baby ocelots afraid to cross the newly striped three-lane road. We left behind the sight of the last ghost bike in town and came across wooden crucifixes that stretched out along the Rio Grande Valley's Highway 69. Finally, another pick-up truck with fruit spilling from all sides and a little boy sitting on a milk crate, daydreaming...his thoughts being carried away on the wings of stingy flies while farmers with mesquite splinters under their nails promised the sweetest summer fruit.

Cholo

"Sometimes the barrio claims us, holds us by our feet like roots in its field of chalk outlines closed off by the screaming yellow tape being pulled from its soul."

There's a cholo in my poems
he wanders and peeks his head in and out
of each stanza

He is walking the straight lines
in my journals
drawing caskets, spray painting the edges,
kissing my girl and making his saliva
drain down her throat
bypassing her heart,
flowing down,
carving his initials in her insides

He lives deep inside
finds corners of her heart
where tears well up before they make
their way out.
He sits with his head down, cap pulled back,
smoking on a cigarette, taking slow drags
blowing heart-shaped smoke rings
towards her baby blue lungs

He runs fast inside of me
pushing through my guts
piercing like a stray bullet.

He skips over pages of my life
written in red ink
inhaling paint fumes through paper bags,
in worn out shoes, mind on his money,
revenge and crying with thoughts of his
madrecita

This cholo reads books,
chews up his fingernails
-spitting into the mulch that covers
the syringes in the playground where
his little sister was kidnapped, and found
days later roaming,
listless, confused, but alive

He sits
on my front porch
with beer cans at his feet
near the puddle of piss
and burnt out joints

he enjoys haikus
that remind him of his love,
summer, acid trips, and sex

He's a cholo
who wanders and intertwines.
Like a pantoum of veins in my stomach
he caresses my soul

Who wanders and intertwines.
Between life and death
he caresses my soul
leaving me for dead.

Author Biography

Born in Los Angeles in 1973, Edward Vidaurre now works and resides in the Río Grande Valley. His poetry has been published in multiple venues, including *riverSedge, La Bloga, Bordersenses, La Noria, Left Hand of the Father, Voices de la Luna, Brooklyn & Boyle, ¡Juventud! Growing up along the Border*, and the *Boundless* Anthology of the Valley International Poetry Festival. His previous books are *I Took My Barrio on a Road Trip* (Slough Press. 2013), *Insomnia* (El Zarape Press, 2014), and *Beautiful Scars: Elegiac Beat Poems* (El Zarape Press, 2015).

other titles from

FlowerSong Books &

Juventud Press

Transplant

Poems by Shirley Ricket.

ISBN: 978-0692354339

FlowerSong Books

Where is home? Mostly in the mind and spirit. If we visit a place where once we lived, it's the memories crowding in that take us back, not the plaster and brick. Moving is in our DNA, even if we have lived in the same place for years. The wood and glass changes because we change. In The Poetics of Space, Gaston Bachelard says that all inhabited space bears a notion of home, and that an entire past comes to dwell in a new abode. Transplant explores these themes of change and loss, and aging, and more. It seeks to carry out what Bachelard calls the function of poetry: "to give us back the situations of our dreams."

La espiral de la locura

Alejandro Cabada

ISBN: 978-0692411520

FlowerSong Books

Quince cuentos de una de las imaginaciones más singulares de la literatura oscura. Una travesía a lo desconocido. Un viaje escalofriante a lo fantástico. Un salto tenebroso al vacío psicodélico de las emociones fuertes. Alejandro Cabada te acompaña al dominio de lo onírico, donde todas las leyes de lo establecido son destruidas y no hay tiempo ni espacio para meditarlo. Abróchate el cinturón. La espiral comienza a girar.

Heartbeat of the Soul of the World
Stories by René Saldaña, Jr.

ISBN: 9780692412039

Juventud Press

A young man finds his voice in jazz, leaving a mark on his community that will never be erased. Another discovers his words in books and carves them into angry poems. Bullied kids at the end of their rope are given friendship and protection, while other teens cannot clear the hurdles life sets in their way. And at every step the promise of love glows bright even in the gloom of teenage life. In this new collection, René Saldaña, Jr., echoes the rhythmic pulse of life along the border. These brave, nuanced, accessible stories—ten previously published and five new—will resonate with young readers everywhere, especially Latinos. Come. Lean in close. Listen to the heartbeat of the soul of the world.

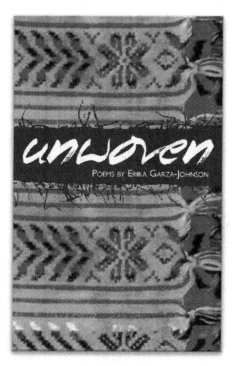

Unwoven
Poems by Erika Garza-Johnson
ISBN: 9780692323908
FlowerSong Books

The first poetry book from one of the most distinctive voices in South
Texas, *Unwoven* is an unflinchingly honest exploration of Chicana
womanhood along the border, a scattering of quetzal feathers and jade that
celebrate the achingly lovely paradox of life on the edges and in the middle.
Playful, artful, and wholly memorable, these poems prove Erika Garza-
Johnson deserving of her enduring moniker: *La Poeta Power.*

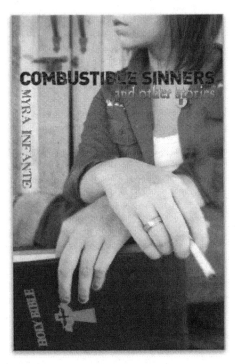

Combustible Sinners and Other Stories
by Myra Infante
ISBN: 9780615556703

Lissi Linares is a pastor's daughter whose love for others contrasts with her fear of eternal damnation. Little Jasmine "Jazzy Moon" Luna is determined to save Jesus from being crucified. Naida Cervantes hides a brutal secret behind shapeless, florid dresses. Hermana Gracie tries to set her son up with a good Christian girlfriend, only to make a surprising discovery. Zeke wants a new guitar and Ben wants a cool girlfriend, but what they find as migrant workers in Arkansas changes their desires. These individuals and others try to negotiate the often rocky intersection of faith and culture in seven independent but intertwining tales that explore life in an evangelical Christian, Mexican-American community. Frank, funny and heart-breakingly real, this volume explores themes of identity, culture, religion and sexuality in the context of a little-known subset of Hispanic culture.

***¡Juventud!* Growing up on the Border**
Edited by René Saldaña, Jr., and Erika Garza-Johnson
ISBN: 9780615778259

Borders are magical places, and growing up on a border, crossing and recrossing that space where this becomes that, creates a very special sort of person, one in whom multiple cultures, languages, identities and truths mingle in powerful ways. In these eight stories and sixteen poems, a wide range of authors explore issues that confront young people along the US-Mexico border, helping their unique voices to be heard and never ignored.

Featuring the work of David Rice, Xavier Garza, Jan Seale, Guadalupe García McCall, Diane Gonzales Bertrand, and many others.

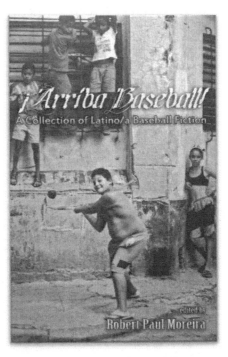

¡Arriba Baseball! A Collection of Latino/a Baseball Fiction
Edited by Robert Paul Moreira
ISBN: 9780615781839

From Dodger Stadium to the Astrodome, from the Río Grande Valley to Chicago, from Veracruz to Puerto Rico, from high-school teams to stickball in the streets, from the lessons of fathers to the excited joy of daughters, from massive cheering in the stands at Wrigley Field to the dynamics of family and community echoing on the diamond, these fifteen stories use the sport of baseball to explore geographical, cultural and dream-like spaces that transcend traditional notions of the game and transform it into a universal yet wholly individual experience.

Featuring the work of Dagoberto Gilb, Norma Elia Cantú, Nelson Denis, Christine Granados, René Saldaña, Jr., and many more.

Mexican Bestiary | Bestiario Mexicano
by David Bowles and Noé Vela
ISBN: 9780615571195

Who protects our precious fields of corn? What leaps from the darkness when you least suspect it? Which spirit waits for little kids by rivers and lakes? From the ahuizotl to the xocoyoles——and all the imps, ghosts and witches in between——this illustrated bilingual encyclopedia tells you just what you need to know about the things that go bump in the night in Mexico and the US Southwest.

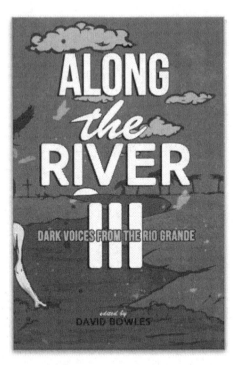

Along the River III: Dark Voices from the Río Grande
Edited by David Bowles
ISBN: 978-0615956183

The third anthology in the *Along the River* series.

When the sun sets on the Río Grande Valley, all manner of dark voices begin to croak, snarl and wail. Come explore the black shadows amidst the mesquite and palm trees down at the water's edge...just have a care not to fall (or be pulled) into the current.

Featuring the short story "Niño" by Álvaro Rodríguez.

FLOWERSONG BOOKS nurtures essential words from the border-lands. The imprint is named for the Nahuatl phrase *in xōchitl in cuīcatl*—literally "the flower, the song," a kenning for "poetry."

Our mission is to promote both the voices of writers in the Río Grande Valley and the literacy of Latinas and Latinos in general. To achieve these goals, we are implementing a multi-tiered strategy:

- editing an annual anthology of local talent (*Along the River* is the name of this series)
- publishing a small number of titles by Valley authors (or by authors whose work would appeal to readers in the Valley) each year
- procuring top-notch authors to edit anthologies of established and upcoming writers whose work has special relevance to the Río Grande Valley
- providing creative writing workshops to aspiring local writers
- conducting writing contests for elementary and secondary children

Made in the USA
Charleston, SC
26 August 2016